A
Spicing
of Birds

A Driftless Series Book

This book is the
2010 selection in the
Driftless New England
category, for a
poetry book by a
New England
author.

A Spicing of Birds

POEMS BY EMILY DICKINSON

Poems for birders selected and
introduced by Jo Miles Schuman
and Joanna Bailey Hodgman with
illustrations by eighteenth- and
nineteenth-century bird artists

WESLEYAN UNIVERSITY PRESS | MIDDLETOWN, CONNECTICUT

Wesleyan University Press

Middletown CT 06459

www.wesleyan.edu/wespress

© 2010 Jo Miles Schuman and Joanna Bailey Hodgman

Printed in China

Library of Congress Cataloging-in-Publication Data

Dickinson, Emily, 1830–1886.

   A spicing of birds: poems / by Emily Dickinson; poems for birders selected and introduced by Jo Miles Schuman and Joanna Bailey Hodgman with illustrations by eighteenth- and nineteenth-century bird artists.

   p. cm. — (A Driftless series book)

Includes bibliographical references and index.

ISBN 978-0-8195-7069-7 (cloth: alk. paper)

1. Birds — Poetry.   I. Schuman, Jo Miles.

II. Hodgman, Joanna Bailey.   III. Title.

PS1541.A6   2010a

811'.4 — dc22   2010007203

5 4 3

The Driftless Series is funded by the
Beatrice Fox Auerbach Foundation Fund
at the Hartford Foundation for Public Giving.

For Howard, Marc, Beth, and David
&
For Kit, our children, our grandchildren,
and my brother Chuck

In memory of M.B.M. and D.W.B.

Contents

Illustrations

"A View from the East of the Dickinson
Home as It Appears Today; the Boxed
Garden is Where the Orchard Was in Emily's
Day." Illustration from Josephine Pollitt,
*Emily Dickinson: The Human Background of Her
Poetry,* 1930, photographer unknown.

Introduction

Emily Dickinson, Intimate of Birds

Yet was not the foe — of any —
Not the smallest Bird
In the nearest Orchard dwelling
Be of Me — afraid.

In those four short lines, in her own unusual word order, the poet
Emily Dickinson summed up her closeness with birds. Put in more
ordinary prose: Not even the smallest bird in her orchard need feel
afraid of her. In his essay "What Are You Really?" Roger Tory Peterson
struggled over what to call people fascinated by birds. He asked: "Are
you a bird watcher, ornithologist, ornithophile, an aviphile, a bird
lover, bird fancier, bird bander, birder, bird spotter, lister, ticker [list
maker], twitcher [pursuer of rare birds] — or what?"[1] Dickinson falls
into the categories of bird watcher and bird lover, and we would add
bird listener and "intimate of birds."

According to a recent survey conducted by the U.S. Fish and Wild-
life Service, 46 million people in the United States enjoy watching
birds. Of these, only about one person in eight can identify more than
twenty species, so the large majority probably consists of home bird-
ers: people who maintain bird feeders and enjoy seeing and identifying
the birds in their own yards.[2] This was the case with Dickinson, and
although she mentioned twenty-six species specifically in her poems,
given her interest, she may have known many more by name.

Born December 10, 1830, Dickinson lived in Amherst, Massachusetts, all her life and rarely left home. Educated at Amherst Academy and Mary Lyon's Female Seminary (now Mount Holyoke College), she became something of a recluse in later life and distilled her observations and philosophy into succinct poems. Current anthologies date her first poem as written in 1850, when she was twenty, and her last in 1886, the year she died at fifty-six. They are original, spare, and highly idiosyncratic poems. Receiving little notice during her lifetime, only a few were published. She did, however, send poems to friends in letters, or to accompany gifts of flowers. They became more widely known soon after her death, and she is now one of America's most revered poets. She very rarely titled her poems, and they are referred to in this introduction by their number in *The Complete Poems of Emily Dickinson*, edited by Thomas H. Johnson. Johnson arranged them in what he believed from his research to be the chronological order of their composition. A more recent compilation, *The Poems of Emily Dickinson*, edited by R. W. Franklin, numbers the poems differently. We have included both sets of numbers under each poem in the body of this book; for example the poem beginning "The Judge is like the Owl" is referred to as J [for Johnson] 699/ F [for Franklin] 728.[3]

Dickinson lived on her father's small farm — a fourteen-acre property with a barn, extensive perennial gardens, an orchard, vegetable garden, fields, and woods. This variety of habitats sheltered many birds. She observed them closely and knew intimately their songs, habits, and characteristics. Some of these species are rare around homes in New England today — bobolinks, whippoorwills, meadowlarks, bluebirds, and cuckoos suffered loss of habitat as large developments replaced fields and orchards. On the other hand, Dickinson may have seldom seen cardinals and mockingbirds, as these were infrequent visitors in the Northeast during her lifetime, before global warming pushed their range northward.

No pocket guides to birds were available in Dickinson's day. Although ornithologists published their findings from the beginning of the European settlement of America, popular bird identification books for the general public were not produced until almost the end of the nineteenth century. In 1832, Thomas Nuttall published a book for this purpose illustrated with woodcuts, but it was hardly a concise field guide — it numbered eight hundred pages.[4]

Our selection of Dickinson's poems is illustrated with the work of eight artist/ornithologists, all but one of whom lived at least part of their lives during the nineteenth century. The exception is Mark Catesby, who lived in the late seventeenth to mid-eighteenth century. These artists were chosen to show the variety and high quality of bird art over this time span. Dickinson may have been familiar with the work of five of them: Mark Catesby, Alexander Wilson, John James Audubon, John H. Hall, and Robert Ridgway. Some of the books they illustrated might well have been in the libraries of the schools she attended. (Brief biographical sketches of these pioneers of American bird illustration are included in the Appendix.) Careful study of the illustrations will find similarities among them. For instance, to illustrate the phoebe subject of Dickinson's poem J1009 (page 47), we selected a color lithograph that Montague Chamberlain added to his much later revised edition (1903) of Thomas Nuttall's 1832 *A Manual of the Ornithology of the United States and Canada*. However, in the same illustration you can see a song sparrow that clearly is an unacknowledged copy of Ridgway's lithograph (1875) shown in the illustration for poem J1761 (page 41). Perhaps it was with Ridgway's permission, but possibly not. This kind of appropriation was not uncommon at the time and seems to have been tolerated. John James Audubon copied some of Wilson's birds without giving credit.[5] Moreover, some of the early work of these artists was often a collaboration with engravers, colorists (who filled in the engravings by hand), and other assistants.

Dickinson's collected poems include 222 that make references to birds. Birds are woven through her poems like the string she mentions that "Robins steal . . . for Nests —."[6] Or perhaps we could say that her poems have "a spicing of Birds," a phrase she used in describing the natural environment.[7] She was a keen observer and often captures the essence of a bird with her words: "Before you thought of Spring . . . a Fellow in the Skies" (the bluebird, first to return); the "sweet derision of the crow"; "the new Robin's ecstasy"; "mad and sweet — as a Mob of Bobolinks."[8] She knew their different habitats, mentioning birds of the meadows, woods, orchard, barn, lawns, and gardens. She was aware of their seasonal comings and goings. In a letter from Cambridge to her sister-in-law, Susan Gilbert Dickinson, in September 1864, she asked "Are the Apples ripe — Have the Wild Geese crossed — ?"[9]

We have selected poems for this collection that show Dickinson's acute perceptions of the habits and qualities of the birds she knew. We also tried to represent as many species as possible, although in the case of some of her favorites — robins, hummingbirds, and orioles among them — they appear more than once, with a different focus in each poem. Taken as a whole, these poems put Dickinson in the class of skilled and experienced birders and reflect the many attributes of birds. Birds are part of the earth and of the sky; their songs can seem both natural and ethereal; their behavior both defines them and suggests similar aspects of human behavior. The poems also reflect Dickinson's fondness for contrasts: between religion and nature, optimism and pessimism, shyness and self-confidence, life and death.

Dickinson tells us, "Some keep the Sabbath going to Church — / I keep it, staying at Home — / With a Bobolink for a Chorister —."[10] Emphasizing optimism, she writes of the bluebird: "Her conscientious Voice will soar unmoved / Above ostensible Vicissitude."[11] In contrast, however, she says, "One Joy of so much anguish / Sweet nature has for me . . . Why Birds, a Summer morning / . . . Should stab my ravished spirit / With Dirks of Melody."[12] Defining her own shyness, Dickinson gives us the phoebe and the wren: "I dwelt too low that any seek — / Too shy, that any blame — / A Phoebe makes a little print / Upon the floors of Fame —."[13] And "For every Bird a Nest — / Wherefore in timid quest / Some little Wren goes seeking round —."[14] On the other hand, the raucous blue jay provides opposing behavior: "The Jay his Castanet has struck."[15] In winter, "the Jay will giggle / At his new white House the Earth."[16] And the hummingbird becomes a giddy cyclist: "Within my Garden, rides a Bird / Upon a single wheel —."[17] In addition, some bird songs create a mixture of emotions in the listener. Although they often bring joy and rising spirits, occasionally the songs emphasize the grief and silence of death: "The saddest noise, the sweetest noise, / The maddest noise that grows, — / The birds, they make it in the spring, / . . . It makes us think of all the dead / That sauntered with us here, / By separation's sorcery / Made cruelly more dear."[18]

These examples show only some of Emily Dickinson's characteristic approaches and subjects in her bird poems. The reader also notes and appreciates poems that focus simply on close descriptions; imagery and metaphor make these descriptions vibrant. Observing an owl, she notes, "The Judge is like the Owl —."[19] Of the woodpecker she writes,

"His Bill an Auger is."[20] And she tells us that "The Way to know the Bobolink" is "Precisely as the Joy of him—."[21]

The Dickinson family fed the birds that lived near their house and barn. No commercial bird seed as we know it today was available, but in her poems and letters Dickinson often mentions giving them "crumbs," which seems to indicate smallness of particle, not necessarily bread crumbs. In a letter to Mrs. Samuel Bowles, probably written June 18, 1880, Dickinson described how her father fed the birds during an April snowstorm the previous year: "the birds were so frightened and cold they sat by the kitchen door. Father went to the barn in his slippers and came back with a breakfast of grain for each, and hid himself while he scattered it, lest it embarrass them . . . their descendants are singing this afternoon."[22] She also wrote to thank Elizabeth Carmichael for a "little tub," which she "shall keep till the birds [come], filling it then with nectars" presumably for hummingbirds.[23] Dickinson realized the need to provide birds with water during a heat wave: "We have an artificial Sea and to see the Birds follow the Hose for a Crumb of Water is a touching Sight. They wont take it if I hand it to them—they run and shriek as if they were being assassinated, but oh, to steal it, that is bliss."[24]

Dickinson seemed to be most deeply affected by bird song. In an unfinished fragment she wrote: "One note from one Bird / Is better than a million words / A scabbard holds (has-needs) but one sword."[25] She was so sensitive to bird song that it seemed to be an almost physical assault: "And then he lifted up his Throat / And squandered such a Note / A Universe that overheard / Is stricken by it yet—."[26] Although many of her poems mention bird songs without being clear as to species, she does refer to the calls and songs of the [meadow] lark, blue jay, robin, bluebird, plover, oriole, bobolink, blackbird, phoebe, whippoorwill, and cuckoo. She knew their unique vocalizations: "the Jays bark like Blue Terriers" she wrote to a friend.[27] In a letter to Jane Humphrey, a former schoolmate, in the spring of 1852, a young Dickinson wrote: "I do wish I could tell you just how the Robins sang — they dont sing now, because it is past their bedtime, and they're all fast asleep, but they *did* sing, this morning, for when we were going to church, they filled the air with such melody, and sang so deliciously, that I tho't really, Jennie, I never should get to meeting."[28] Dickinson knew, as all dedicated birders do, that you have to rise early to hear the great spring chorus of returning birds:

> The Birds begun at Four o'clock —
> Their period for Dawn —
> A Music numerous as space —
> But neighboring as Noon — [29]

And she observed changes in the quality of their songs. In a letter to her brother Austin she wrote: "The air was really scorching, the sun red and hot, and you know just how the birds sing before a thunder storm, a sort of hurried, and agitated song — pretty soon it began to thunder . . . then came the wind and rain."[30]

The welfare of the birds concerned her from an early age. In a letter to Abiah Root in February 1845, a fifteen-year-old Emily described unusual May-like weather unlike "arctic February" and then wrote: "I have heard some sweet little birds sing, but I fear we shall have more cold weather and their little bills will be frozen up before their songs are finished."[31]

Well into the late 1890s, any serious study of birds entailed shooting specimens by the thousands; ornithologists, bird artists, and amateur collectors all thought it necessary. Moreover, bird feathers were in great demand to decorate women's hats. Some birds, such as egrets, were threatened with extinction. At its height, in the late 1890s, the feather trade was killing an estimated 200 million birds a year.[32]

Emily Dickinson was ahead of her time in being outraged by the act of killing birds with a gun. Her poem J1102, written around 1866, is a powerful testament to her horror at this practice:

> . . . to be
> Assassin of a Bird
> Resembles to my outraged mind
> The firing in Heaven,
> On Angels — squandering for you
> Their Miracles of Tune —[33]

Other writers, among them Henry David Thoreau, Celia Thaxter, and Sara Orne Jewett, also addressed this issue early on.

In 1889, Florence Merriam Bailey wrote *Birds through an Opera Glass*.[34] This portable book and the use of binoculars made it possible to identify birds in the field without first shooting them. It described seventy species and was considered the first useful field guide, but this was three years after Dickinson's death. Bailey's book was instrumental in furthering a growing interest in bird watching by the general public.[35]

The advent of photography also aided in nondestructive bird identification and study. Cordelia Stanwood (1865–1958), of Ellsworth, Maine, was not above wearing hip rubber boots under her long skirts as she went out hunting for birds in the swamps and woods, carrying a heavy camera, tripod, and glass plates to document them in their natural habitats. Through her long, patient hours of observation, she was able to locate a large number of nests; the nests and young birds became her specialty. Her observations and photographs were used by

"Six Little Chickadees," photograph by Cordelia J. Stanwood.

> Men are picking up the apples to-day, and the pretty
> boarders are leaving the trees . . . I have heard a chipper
> say 'dee' six times in disapprobation. How should we like
> to have our privileges wheeled away in a barrel?
> — From a letter to Louise Norcross, early September 1880,
>   in Dickinson, *Letters of Emily Dickinson*, 3:670.

well-known bird authorities in their books, as well as in her own pub-
lished articles.[36]

In the 1880s, prominent ornithologists began to be concerned about
the slaughter. George Bird Grinnell, who founded the first Audubon
Society in 1886, the year Dickinson died, was an early conservationist
trying to end the market for eggs, birds, and feathers. Members of the
society, by the thousands, signed a pledge to work against the destruc-
tion of birds and eggs. However, although the Audubon Society had

many enthusiastic members, it was financially unstable, and Grinnell gave up. He had made no progress against the use of bird feathers or other slaughter for market, and the organization folded.[37] Frank Chapman, although an avid hunter, was also an early conservationist. In 1900, he initiated the still-popular annual Christmas Bird Count to replace the holiday tradition of a "match hunt" in which the largest pile of dead birds and animals won.[38]

When these and other prominent, deeply concerned ornithologists failed to stop the slaughter, women took on the task. In 1896, after she read an account concerning the killing of herons and egrets for millinery, Harriet Lawrence Hemenway organized a group of women who created the Massachusetts Audubon Society. Soon chapters spread to other states. Through education, pressure, and example, they were able to stem the tide; the first federal protective legislation was passed in 1900. Further legislation in 1913 shut down the feather industry and protected all migrating birds.[39] Emily Dickinson, had she lived into her eighties, would have rejoiced.

Susan Dickinson wrote in her obituary for Dickinson: "So intimate and passionate was her love of Nature, she seemed herself a part of the high March sky, the summer day and bird-call."[40]

Birds were an inseparable part of Dickinson's world. She brings them to us in her poetry, where we see and hear them through her eyes and ears. Her brilliant observations enrich our own acquaintance with these same "common" birds. Many readers familiar with the songs of birds but less so with the cadences of poetry may find unexpected beauty and pleasure in her words.

Jo Miles Schuman   Joanna Bailey Hodgman
Phippsburg, Maine   Rochester, New York

Notes

Emily Dickinson, *The Complete Poems of Emily Dickinson*, ed. Thomas H. Johnson (Boston: Little, Brown and Company, 1960), J925. Unless otherwise indicated, references to all poems in this book are from this edition, and are hereafter referred to by number and first line.

1. Roger Tory Peterson, "What Are You Really," in *All Things Reconsidered: My Birding Adventures*, ed. Bill Thompson III, 10–19 (New York: Houghton Mifflin, 2006). Reprinted from *Bird Watcher's Digest* (March/April 1984).
2. Scott Weidensaul, *Of a Feather: A Brief History of American Birding* (Orlando, Fla.: Harcourt Books, 2007), 297.
3. Emily Dickinson, *The Poems of Emily Dickinson*, ed. R. W. Franklin (Cambridge, Mass.: Belknap Press of Harvard University Press, 2005).
4. Weidensaul, *Of a Feather*, 86; Thomas Nuttall, *A Manual of the Ornithology of the United States and Canada* (Cambridge: Hilliard and Brown, 1832).
5. Weidensaul, *Of a Feather*, 86 and 191; Felton Gibbons and Deborah Strom, *Neighbors to the Birds: A History of Birdwatching in America* (New York: W.W. Norton, 1988), 57.
6. Letter to Samuel Bowles, early summer, 1862, in Emily Dickinson, *The Letters of Emily Dickinson*, ed. Thomas H. Johnson (Cambridge, Mass.: Belknap Press of Harvard University Press, 1958), 2:410. Hereafter referred to as *Letters*.
7. Letter to Samuel Bowles, late August 1858(?), in *Letters*, 1:339.
8. J1465, "Before you thought of Spring"; J1669, "In snow thou comest"; J128, "Bring me the sunset in a cup"; Letter to Martha Dickinson, about 1883, in *Letters*, 3:787.
9. Letter to Susan Gilbert Dickinson, September 1864, in *Letters*, 2:434.
10. J324, "Some keep the Sabbath going to Church."
11. J1395, "After all Birds have been investigated and laid aside."
12. J1420, "One Joy of so much anguish."
13. J1009, "I was a phoebe — nothing more."
14. J143, "For every Bird a Nest."
15. J1635, "The Jay his Castanet has struck."
16. J1381, "I suppose the time will come."

17. J500, "Within my Garden, rides a Bird."

18. J1764, "The saddest noise, the sweetest noise."

19. J699, "The Judge is like the Owl."

20. J1034, "His Bill an Auger is."

21. J1279, "The Way to know the Bobolink."

22. Letter to Mrs. Samuel Bowles, June 1880(?), in *Letters*, 3:662.

23. Letter to Elizabeth Carmichael, early 1884(?), *Letters*, 3:809.

24. Letter to Mrs. J. G. Holland, August 1881, in *Letters*, 3:706.

25. Included in the appendix of Prose Fragments, under "Aphorisms," number 97, in *Letters*, 3:926; reprinted from *The New England Quarterly* (September 1955): 316.

26. J1600, "Upon his Saddle sprung a Bird."

27. Letter to Mrs. J. G. Holland, early March 1866, in *Letters*, 2:449.

28. Letter to Jane Humphrey, about April 1852, in *Letters*, 1:198. Here, as elsewhere in letters and poems, words are spelled as Dickinson wrote them.

29. J783, "The Birds begun at Four o'clock."

30. Letter to Austin Dickinson, 10 May 1852, in *Letters*, 1:204.

31. Letter to Abiah Root, 23 February 1845, in *Letters*, 1:9.

32. Weidensaul, *Of a Feather*, 151.

33. J1102, "His Bill is clasped — his Eye forsook."

34. Florence Merriam Bailey, *Birds through an Opera Glass* (New York: Chautauqua Press, 1889).

35. Weidensaul, *Of a Feather*, 134.

36. Chandler S. Richmond, *Beyond the Spring: Cordelia J. Stanwood of Birdsacre, New and Revised Edition* (Ellsworth, Maine: The Latona Press, 1989, and Ellsworth, Maine: Downeast Graphics and Printing Inc., 2008).

37. Weidensaul, *Of a Feather*, 152–53.

38. Ibid., 148–49.

39. Ibid., 155–61.

40. Ellen Louise Hart and Martha Nell Smith, eds., *Open Me Carefully: Emily Dickinson's Intimate Letters to Susan Huntington Dickinson* (Ashfield, Mass.: Paris Press, 1998), 267.

A
Spicing
of Birds

1.

2.

3.

95.

Common Blue Bird

1. Male. 2. Female. 3 Young.

Great Mullein Verbascum Thapsus.

Before you thought of Spring
Except as a Surmise
You see — God bless his suddenness —
A Fellow in the Skies
Of independent Hues
A little weather worn
Inspiriting habiliments
Of Indigo and Brown —
With specimens of Song
As if for you to choose —
Discretion in the interval
With gay delays he goes
To some superior Tree
Without a single Leaf
And shouts for joy to Nobody
But his seraphic self —

J1465/F1484

1. *Turdus Melodus*, Wood Thrush. 2. *Turdus Migratorius*, Red-breasted Thrush, or Robin.
3. *Sitta Carolinensis*, White-breasted black-capped Nuthatch. 4. *Sitta Varia*, Red-bellied-black-capped Nuthatch.

The Robin is the One
That interrupt the Morn
With hurried — few — express Reports
When March is scarcely on —

The Robin is the One
That overflow the Noon
With her cherubic quantity —
An April but begun —

The Robin is the One
That speechless from her Nest
Submit that Home — and Certainty
And Sanctity, are best

J828/F501

American Robin, or Migratory Thrush.
Male 1. Female 2 and young
Chesnut Oak. Quercus prinus.

The Robin is a Gabriel
In humble circumstances —
His Dress denotes him socially,
Of Transport's Working Classes —
He has the punctuality
Of the New England Farmer —
The same oblique integrity,
A Vista vastly warmer —

A small but sturdy Residence,
A self denying Household,
The Guests of Perspicacity
Are all that cross his Threshold —
As covert as a Fugitive,
Cajoling Consternation
By Ditties to the Enemy
And Sylvan Punctuation —

J1483/F1520

If I shouldn't be alive
When the Robins come,
Give the one in Red Cravat,
A Memorial crumb.

If I couldn't thank you,
Being fast asleep,
You will know I'm trying
With my Granite lip!

J182/F210

The Way to know the Bobolink
From every other Bird
Precisely as the Joy of him —
Obliged to be inferred.

Of impudent Habiliment
Attired to defy,
Impertinence subordinate
At times to Majesty.

Of Sentiments seditious
Amenable to Law —
As Heresies of Transport
Or Puck's Apostacy.

Extrinsic to Attention
Too intimate with Joy —
He compliments existence
Until allured away

By Seasons or his Children —
Adult and urgent grown —
Or unforeseen aggrandizement
Or, happily, Renown —

By Contrast certifying
The Bird of Birds is gone —
How nullified the Meadow —
Her Sorcerer withdrawn!

J1279/F1348

Wandering Rice bird.

1. Male 2. Female
Red Maple. Acer Rubrum.

No Bobolink — reverse His Singing
When the only Tree
Ever He minded occupying
By the Farmer be —

Clove to the Root —
His Spacious Future —
Best Horizon — gone —
Whose Music be His
Only Anodyne —
Brave Bobolink —

J755/F766

Great Horned-Owl.

The Judge is like the Owl —
I've heard my Father tell —
And Owls do build in Oaks —
So here's an Amber Sill —

That slanted in my Path —
When going to the Barn —
And if it serve You for a House —
Itself is not in vain —

About the price — 'tis small —
I only ask a Tune
At Midnight — Let the Owl select
His favorite Refrain.

J699/F728

The Bird her punctual music brings
And lays it in its place —
Its place is in the Human Heart
And in the Heavenly Grace —
What respite from her thrilling toil
Did Beauty ever take —
But Work might be electric Rest
To those that Magic make —

J1585/F1556

Some keep the Sabbath going to Church —
I keep it, staying at Home —
With a Bobolink for a Chorister —
And an Orchard, for a Dome —

Some keep the Sabbath in Surplice —
I just wear my Wings —
And instead of tolling the Bell, for Church,
Our little Sexton — sings.

God preaches, a noted Clergyman —
And the sermon is never long,
So instead of getting to Heaven, at last —
I'm going, all along.

J324/F236

BOB-O-LINK.

(Dolichonyx oryzivorus.)

Adult male, in Spring.

His Bill is clasped — his Eye forsook —
His Feathers wilted low —
The Claws that clung, like lifeless Gloves
Indifferent hanging now —
The Joy that in his happy Throat
Was waiting to be poured
Gored through and through with Death, to be
Assassin of a Bird
Resembles to my outraged mind
The firing in Heaven,
On Angels — squandering for you
Their Miracles of Tune —

J1102/F1126

High from the earth I heard a bird,
He trod upon the trees
As he esteemed them trifles,
And then he spied a breeze,
And situated softly
Upon a pile of wind
Which in a perturbation
Nature had left behind.
A joyous going fellow
I gathered from his talk
Which both of benediction
And badinage partook.
Without apparent burden
I subsequently learned
He was the faithful father
Of a dependent brood.
And this untoward transport
His remedy for care.
A contrast to our respites.
How different we are!

J1723/F1778

Split the Lark — and you'll find the Music —
Bulb after Bulb, in Silver rolled —
Scantily dealt to the Summer Morning
Saved for your Ear when Lutes be old.

Loose the Flood — you shall find it patent —
Gush after Gush, reserved for you —
Scarlet Experiment! Sceptic Thomas!
Now, do you doubt that your Bird was true?

J861/F905

1. *Corvus cristatus.* Blue Jay. 2. *Fringilla Tristis,* Yellow-Bird or Goldfinch.

3. *Oriolus Baltimorus,* Baltimore Bird.

No Brigadier throughout the Year
So civic as the Jay —
A Neighbor and a Warrior too
With shrill felicity
Pursuing Winds that censure us
A February Day,
The Brother of the Universe
Was never blown away —
The Snow and he are intimate —
I've often seen them play
When Heaven looked upon us all
With such severity
I felt apology were due
To an insulted sky
Whose pompous frown was Nutriment
To their Temerity —
The Pillow of this daring Head
Is pungent Evergreens —
His Larder — terse and Militant —
Unknown — refreshing things —
His Character — a Tonic —
His Future — a Dispute —
Unfair an Immortality
That leaves this Neighbor out —

J1561/F1596

Louis Agassiz Fuertes

His Bill an Auger is
His Head, a Cap and Frill
He laboreth at every Tree
A Worm, His utmost Goal.

J1034/F990

All the letters I can write
Are not fair as this —
Syllables of Velvet —
Sentences of Plush,
Depths of Ruby, undrained,
Hid, Lip, for Thee —
Play it were a Humming Bird —
And just sipped — me —

J334/F380

RUBY-THROATED HUMMING-BIRD.

Within my Garden, rides a Bird
Upon a single Wheel —
Whose spokes a dizzy Music make
As 'twere a travelling Mill —

He never stops, but slackens
Above the Ripest Rose —
Partakes without alighting
And praises as he goes,

Till every spice is tasted —
And then his Fairy Gig
Reels in remoter atmospheres —
And I rejoin my Dog,

And He and I, perplex us
If positive, 'twere we —
Or bore the Garden in the Brain
This Curiosity —

But He, the best Logician,
Refers my clumsy eye —
To just vibrating Blossoms!
An Exquisite Reply!

J500/F370

A Route of Evanescence
With a revolving Wheel —
A Resonance of Emerald —
A Rush of Cochineal —
And every Blossom on the Bush
Adjusts its tumbled Head —
The mail from Tunis, probably,
An easy Morning's Ride —

J1463/F1489

The Birds begun at Four o'clock —
Their period for Dawn —
A Music numerous as space —
But neighboring as Noon —

I could not count their Force —
Their Voices did expend
As Brook by Brook bestows itself
To multiply the Pond.

Their Witnesses were not —
Except occasional man —
In homely industry arrayed —
To overtake the Morn —

Nor was it for applause —
That I could ascertain —
But independent Ecstasy
Of Deity and Men —

By Six, the Flood had done —
No Tumult there had been
Of Dressing, or Departure —
And yet the Band was gone —

The Sun engrossed the East —
The Day controlled the World —
The Miracle that introduced
Forgotten, as fulfilled.

J783/F504

30

BALTIMORE ORIOLE.

(Icterus baltimore.)

Adult male.

One Joy of so much anguish
Sweet nature has for me
I shun it as I do Despair
Or dear iniquity —
Why Birds, a Summer morning
Before the Quick of Day
Should stab my ravished spirit
With Dirks of Melody
Is part of an inquiry
That will receive reply
When Flesh and Spirit sunder
In Death's Immediately —

J1420/F1450

One of the ones that Midas touched
Who failed to touch us all
Was that confiding Prodigal
The reeling Oriole —

So drunk he disavows it
With badinage divine —
So dazzling we mistake him
For an alighting Mine —

A Pleader — a Dissembler —
An Epicure — a Thief —
Betimes an Oratorio —
An Ecstasy in chief —

The Jesuit of Orchards
He cheats as he enchants
Of an entire Attar
For his decamping wants —

The splendor of a Burmah
The Meteor of Birds,
Departing like a Pageant
Of Ballads and of Bards —

I never thought that Jason sought
For any Golden Fleece
But then I am a rural man
With thoughts that make for Peace —

But if there were a Jason,
Tradition bear with me
Behold his lost Aggrandizement
Upon the Apple Tree —

J1466/F1488

Baltimore Oriole, or Hang-nest

1 Male adult. 2. Young Male. 3 Female.

Tulip Tree.

Drawn from Nature by J.J.Audubon, F.R.S.F.L.S.   Lith.ᵈPrinted & Col.ᵈ by J.T.Bowen, Phil.

To hear an Oriole sing
May be a common thing —
Or only a divine.

It is not of the Bird
Who sings the same, unheard,
As unto Crowd —

The Fashion of the Ear
Attireth that it hear
In Dun, or fair —

So whether it be Rune,
Or whether it be none
Is of within.

The "Tune is in the Tree —"
The Skeptic — showeth me —
"No Sir! In Thee!"

J526/F402

Meadow Starling or Meadow Lark.

1 Males 2 Females and Nest.
Yellow flowered Gerardia.

Drawn from Nature by J. J. Audubon. F.R.S.F.L.S.　　　　　　Lithᵈ Printed & Colᵈ by J. T. Bowen Philad.

For every Bird a Nest —
Wherefore in timid quest
Some little Wren goes seeking round —

Wherefore when boughs are free —
Households in every tree —
Pilgrim be found?

Perhaps a home too high —
Ah Aristocracy!
The little Wren desires —

Perhaps of twig so fine —
Of twine e'en superfine,
Her pride aspires —

The Lark is not ashamed
To build upon the ground
Her modest house —

Yet who of all the throng
Dancing around the sun
Does so rejoice?

J143/F86

A train went through a burial gate,
A bird broke forth and sang,
And trilled, and quivered, and shook his throat
Till all the churchyard rang;

And then adjusted his little notes,
And bowed and sang again.
Doubtless, he thought it meet of him
To say good-by to men.

J1761/F397

SONG SPARROW.

(*Melospiza melodia.*)

Adult.

Conferring with myself
My stranger disappeared
Though first upon a berry fat
Miraculously fared
How paltry looked my cares
My practise how absurd
Superfluous my whole career
Beside this travelling Bird

J1655/F1739

The saddest noise, the sweetest noise,
　　The maddest noise that grows, —
The birds, they make it in the spring,
　　At night's delicious close.

Between the March and April line —
　　That magical frontier
Beyond which summer hesitates,
　　Almost too heavenly near.

It makes us think of all the dead
　　That sauntered with us here,
By separation's sorcery
　　Made cruelly more dear.

It makes us think of what we had,
　　And what we now deplore.
We almost wish those siren throats
　　Would go and sing no more.

An ear can break a human heart
　　As quickly as a spear,
We wish the ear had not a heart
　　So dangerously near.

J1764/F1789

A feather from the Whippoorwill
That everlasting — sings!
Whose galleries — are Sunrise —
Whose Opera — the Springs —
Whose Emerald Nest the Ages spin
Of mellow — murmuring thread —
Whose Beryl Egg, what Schoolboys hunt
In "Recess" — Overhead!

J161/F208

Dickinson left two copies of this poem. One of the manuscripts is titled: "Pine
Bough —"; this may be a clue as to where the feather is lodged. See poem 208 in
the Franklin edition.

Whip-poor-will.

Black Oak or Quercitron. Quercus tinctoria.

I was a Phoebe — nothing more —
A Phoebe — nothing less —
The little note that others dropt
I fitted into place —

I dwelt too low that any seek —
Too shy, that any blame —
A Phoebe makes a little print
Upon the Floors of Fame —

J1009/F1009

1. Snow Bird.
2. Song Sparrow.
3. Phoebe.

4. American Goldfinch.
5. Vesper Sparrow.
6. Towhee.

A Sparrow took a Slice of Twig
And thought it very nice
I think, because his empty Plate
Was handed Nature twice —

Invigorated, waded
In all the deepest Sky
Until his little Figure
Was forfeited away —

J1211/F1257

WHITE-THROATED SPARROW.

(Zonotrichia albicollis.)

Adult male.

Upon his Saddle sprung a Bird
And crossed a thousand Trees
Before a Fence without a Fare
His Fantasy did please
And then he lifted up his Throat
And squandered such a Note
A Universe that overheard
Is stricken by it yet —

J1600/F1663

It is a lonesome Glee —
Yet sanctifies the Mind —
With fair association —
Afar upon the Wind

A Bird to overhear
Delight without a Cause —
Arrestless as invisible —
A matter of the Skies.

J774/F873

The most triumphant Bird I ever knew or met

Embarked upon a twig today

And till Dominion set

I famish to behold so eminent a sight

And sang for nothing scrutable

But intimate Delight.

Retired, and resumed his transitive Estate —

To what delicious Accident

Does finest Glory fit!

J1265/F1285

Pl. 117.

Great Carolina Wren.

1. Male 2. Female.

Dwarf Buck-eye. Æsculus Pavia.

Drawn from Nature by J.J.Audubon. F.R.S.Fl.S.

Lithd. Printed & Cold. by J.T.Bowen, Philad.

A prompt — executive Bird is the Jay —
Bold as a Bailiff's Hymn —
Brittle and Brief in quality —
Warrant in every line —

Sitting a Bough like a Brigadier
Confident and straight —
Much is the mien of him in March
As a Magistrate —

J1177/F1022

Smilax lævis, Salicis folio non
Serrato, baccis nigris

A Bird came down the Walk —
He did not know I saw —
He bit an Angleworm in halves
And ate the fellow, raw,

And then he drank a Dew
From a convenient Grass —
And then hopped sidewise to the Wall
To let a Beetle pass —

He glanced with rapid eyes
That hurried all around —
They looked like frightened Beads, I thought —
He stirred his Velvet Head

Like one in danger, Cautious,
I offered him a Crumb
And he unrolled his feathers
And rowed him softer home —

Than Oars divide the Ocean,
Too silver for a seam —
Or Butterflies, off Banks of Noon
Leap, plashless as they swim.

J328/F359

The common Blue Bird of...
Rubecula Americana coerulea.

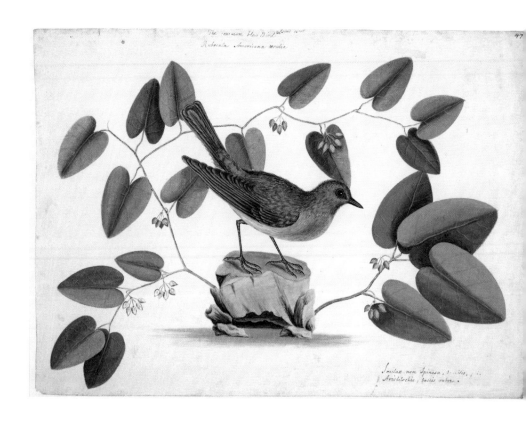

Smilax non Spinosa, ...
Aristolochia, baccis rubra.

After all Birds have been investigated and laid aside —
Nature imparts the little Blue-Bird — assured
Her conscientious Voice will soar unmoved
Above ostensible Vicissitude.

First at the March — competing with the Wind —
Her panting note exalts us — like a friend —
Last to adhere when Summer cleaves away —
Elegy of Integrity.

J1395/F1383

September's Baccalaureate
A combination is
Of Crickets — Crows — and Retrospects
And a dissembling Breeze

That hints without assuming —
An Innuendo sear
That makes the Heart put up its Fun
And turn Philosopher.

J1271/F1313

I suppose the time will come
Aid it in the coming
When the Bird will crowd the Tree
And the Bee be booming.

I suppose the time will come
Hinder it a little
When the Corn in Silk will dress
And in Chintz the Apple

I believe the Day will be
When the Jay will giggle
At his new white House the Earth
That, too, halt a little —

J1381/F1389

Common American Crow.

Male.

Black Walnut.

Drawn from Nature by J. J. Audubon, F.R.S.F.L.S.   Lithd Printed & Cold by J. T. Bowen Phila.

The ones that disappeared are back
The Phoebe and the Crow
Precisely as in March is heard
The curtness of the Jay —
Be this an Autumn or a Spring
My wisdom loses way
One side of me the nuts are ripe
The other side is May.

J1690/F1697

"Hermit Thrush Nest with Four
Eggs and Bunchberry," photograph
by Cordelia J. Stanwood.

For every Bird a Nest —

Biographical Appendix
The Bird Artists

The artists represented in this book are listed in order by date of birth. As noted in the Introduction, although all of them did fine original work, some of them also borrowed occasionally from the art of others, especially when trying to complete a large volume of work. Most of the artists took long, exhausting field trips, exploring wilderness and hunting down (in the early days, literally) the birds of North America. A few also traveled to other parts of the world in their quest for birds.

MARK CATESBY, 1682 – 1749 (pages 55 and 58), was an English naturalist and self-taught artist.[1] From 1712 to 1719, he visited his sister in Virginia and was inspired by the wildlife and plants he saw there. He returned to the area again between 1722 and 1726 to take part in an expedition to southeastern North America and the West Indies. During this time, he collected and preserved plant and bird specimens and also made watercolor paintings. After he returned to England, Catesby wrote and illustrated his book *The Natural History of Carolina, Florida and the Bahama Islands*. It was the first published book to record the flora and fauna of North America, and included plants, mammals, birds, reptiles, amphibians, fish, and invertebrates. The first volume appeared in 1731; the second was completed in 1747. Together, they included 220 plates. The plates in the first volume were etched and hand colored by Catesby himself. In a few cases, he appears to have copied text and illustrations from other naturalists, sometimes without giving credit, but this practice seems to have been common at the time.[2] His style of placing birds in their natural habitat, perched on an accurately drawn plant or tree, later was adopted and developed by John James Audubon. Catesby's book is considered the first American ornithological text and, with its beautiful engravings, was highly successful and widely used — Thomas Jefferson relied on it — until it was superseded by the books of Alexander Wilson and John James Audubon.

ALEXANDER WILSON, 1766–1813 (pages 4 and 22), is sometimes called the "Father of American Ornithology."[3] Born in Scotland, he came to the United States in 1794. He taught school in Pennsylvania, where he met the naturalist William Bartrum. Bartrum fostered Wilson's love of birds and helped him develop his bird identification and drawing skills. Wilson's goal was to publish a book describing and illustrating all the North American birds, and he traveled widely, observing and painting birds. Because printing the book was costly, he learned how to engrave and color his own plates, although later, Alexander Lawson, a Philadelphia engraver, did most of that work. *American Ornithology* was published in nine volumes, from 1808 through 1814. The work illustrates 268 species, including twenty-six that had not been previously recorded. The birds, rather stiff, but in true color, usually were shown in profile, frequently perched on bare branches, with no attempt at careful depiction of specific flora. However, the drawings and written descriptions of the birds were detailed and accurate. Strenuous and extended field trips undermined his health, and Wilson died of dysentery at forty-seven. The eighth and ninth volumes of *American Ornithology* were completed by George Ord after Wilson's death. The book became an important reference for bird watchers for decades, but it was too large to be a field guide.

JOHN JAMES AUDUBON, 1785–1851 (pages 2, 6, 10, 12, 36, 38, 45, 53, and 62), is perhaps America's most celebrated bird illustrator, best known for his monumental book *Birds of America*. He was born in Haiti and grew up in France. Even as a young child, Audubon loved birds; his father encouraged this interest and taught him to appreciate their beauty and observe their behavior.[5] He traveled to the United States in 1803 and lived on a family farm near Philadelphia, studying his natural environment and drawing and painting birds. After many unsuccessful business ventures, he finally determined to surpass Alexander Wilson by creating a more complete book of all North American birds. He went on wide-ranging collecting expeditions and worked intensely on his drawings and paintings. After many setbacks, Audubon completed *Birds of America*. This was published in England over several years, starting in 1827, and it included 497 bird species, depicted life-size with hand-colored etchings based on Audubon's paintings. A smaller octavo edition,[4] from which the illustrations in this book are taken, was published between 1839 and 1844 using a lithographic process. Audubon drew on Wilson for information and evidently copied several of Wilson's drawings without giving credit. He also adapted Catesby's use of accurately drawn plants, but created more complete surroundings and landscapes. Above all, he introduced movement and dramatic action into his scenes. He was less interested in text, and focused his energy and talent on creating extraordinary paintings of the birds he loved so much.

THOMAS NUTTALL, 1786–1859 (pages 26 and 47), was not himself an artist. He was an English botanist and ornithologist who lived in America for most of the years from 1808 to 1842.[6] Soon after arriving in Philadelphia, he met Benjamin Smith Barton, a naturalist and physician, who encouraged his work. In 1811, Nuttall went on the Astor Expedition, which collected plants and birds along the Missouri River. He joined many subsequent expeditions and sometimes set off alone, going on long treks by foot and canoe. Nuttall published several scientific books, mostly botanical, but also *A Manual of the Ornithology of the United States and Canada*, which was illustrated with wood engravings, and published in two volumes in 1832 and 1834. It was written when Nuttall was a member of the faculty at Harvard University (1823–1834) and realized that his students needed something less expensive and more compact than the books of Audubon and Wilson. He borrowed considerably from Wilson's work, however, and did not always give credit.[7] The illustrations for the early editions are thought to be the work of three wood engravers: John H. Hall, Abel Bowen, and Alonzo Hartwell. We have chosen two illustrations from Nuttall's book. One is from the 1832 first edition (see the entry for John H. Hall, below), and one from a much later edition revised and annotated by Montague Chamberlain in 1903. The illustration from the latter, in color lithography, is by an unacknowledged artist (page 47). However, three of the birds in this illustration, the snow bird, song sparrow, and goldfinch, are almost certainly copied from Robert Ridgway. Nuttall's book in both editions was getting closer in format to modern bird identification guides; however, with a very long and detailed text, it was too heavy to be carried easily. Nevertheless, the book still was being used well into the early twentieth century.

JOHN H. HALL (page 26), was born in Cooperstown, New York. He took lessons from Alexander Anderson, the first engraver of wood in America, and began engraving on his own in 1826. Wood engraving is created on the endgrain of a piece of wood, rather than on a flat plank. This means that the tools can be plied in any direction and an engraver can make very fine lines, but the block is usually of small size. Hall first practiced his trade in Albany. Later, in 1830, he was employed by the firm of Carter, Andrews, & Co. of Lancaster, Massachusetts, and then went on to New York. His best engraving is considered to have been for Thomas Nuttall's *A Manual of Ornithology of the United States and Canada*, published in 1832. As was true of most professional wood engravers, he did not design his own blocks. Some of his work was copied from Thomas Bewick, an English engraver, some from Wilson's *American Ornithology*, and some was based on sketches from nature by William Croone. Engraving the sketches probably required much originality on Hall's part. He seemed to move about a lot, and subsequently worked for the Smithsonian Institution in Washington. In 1849, "stricken with gold fever," he went to California, and died there some time later.[8] Although Hall may be considered a craftsman rather than an artist, you can't look at his engravings without feeling a sense of awe and pleasure at his exquisitely fine work. The line between fine art and craft is often blurred.

ROBERT RIDGWAY, 1850–1929 (pages 17, 32, 41, and 49), born in Mount Carmel, Illinois, loved birds from early childhood and was drawing and painting them in his teens.[9] He was a self-taught artist and for many years ground his own pigments. When Ridgway was fourteen, a drawing and inquiry about a bird that he couldn't identify reached Spencer Fullerton Baird at the Smithsonian Institution, and Baird recognized that Ridgway was a prodigy. They kept up a correspondence, and Baird hired him at the age of seventeen to go on an expedition to survey the fortieth parallel as a zoologist. When Ridgway was twenty-two, Baird hired him to work at the Smithsonian.[10] He collaborated with Baird and Thomas Brewer on the five-volume *A History of North American Birds*, first published in 1875. The illustrations as a whole, produced by a chromolithographic process, seem to have been created by several artists and assistants working together. However, Ridgway signed a number of these, so presumably he did the fine drawing on the lithography stone and the hand coloring. Although unacknowledged in the text, some of these same lithographs in a smaller format appear to illustrate Montague Chamberlain's 1903 revision of Nuttall's book *A Popular Handbook of the Birds of the United States and Canada* (see page 47). Ridgway's large original bird paintings were well-known and prized. He published many books and papers; one of the most important was *A Nomenclature of Colors for Naturalists*, a color index to be used in describing birds and animals. Ridgway was curator of birds at the United States National Museum for fifty years, and was a major figure in American ornithology and a founding member of the American Ornithologists' Union.[11]

CORDELIA STANWOOD, 1865–1958 (pages xxi and 64), was born and raised in Ellsworth, Maine.[12] She first attended a teacher-training school and then taught for six years. In 1894, she graduated from the Normal Arts School in Boston and changed her focus to teaching art; for ten years she was supervisor of drawing in several schools, most of them in Massachusetts. Returning home in 1904, Stanwood began an intensive study of native plants and birds, and in 1916 she became a professional photographer. Over a period of thirty-one years, she wrote articles illustrated with her photographs, and published a number in the Audubon Society's *Bird-Lore*, as well as in other magazines, including *The Auk*, the publication of the American Ornithologists' Union.[13] Several of her photographs of nests and young birds are included in the volumes of Edward Howe Forbush's *Birds of Massachusetts and Other New England States*, illustrated by Allen Brooks and Louis Agassiz Fuertes. A large manuscript of her observations and many photographs remain unpublished. After her death at the age of ninety-three, interested townspeople wanting to preserve her legacy purchased her home, which is now the Stanwood Homestead Museum. Her woods and trails are maintained, a bird care facility has been established, and further purchases created the 200-acre Stanwood Wildlife Sanctuary, open to the public.

ALLAN BROOKS, 1869–1946 (pages 15, 31, and 56), was born in India, received his education in England, and then moved with his family to Canada.[14] He became a celebrated ornithologist and self-taught bird artist, traveling widely throughout the world, collecting and drawing. He lived in a cabin on Okanagan Lake, British Columbia. His paintings are in many collections and books, including Taverner's *Birds of Western Canada*, 1926. He also illustrated a field guide, *The Book of Birds*, by Gilbert Grosvenor and Alexander Wetmor, with 950 plates created from his watercolors, which was published by the National Geographic Society. After the death of Louis Agassiz Fuertes (see next entry), Brooks created twenty-four paintings to complete volume 3 of Edward Howe Forbush's *Birds of Massachusetts and Other New England States*.

LOUIS AGASSIZ FUERTES, 1874–1927 (pages 21, 24, and 28), was an ornithologist, illustrator, and artist.[15] He attended Cornell University and began working on commissioned illustrations of birds while still an undergraduate. He traveled all over the world, starting with an expedition down the Alaskan coastline with Edward H. Harriman in 1899. Collaborating with Frank Chapman, Curator of the American Museum of Natural History in New York, Fuertes painted backgrounds to dioramas and engaged in field research, taking part in many expeditions. From 1904 to 1927, his paintings illustrated *Bird Lore*, a popular magazine for birders, founded by Chapman. Fuertes illustrated several books, among them Edward Howe Forbush's three-volume *Birds of Massachusetts and Other New England States*. Tragically, he was killed in an automobile accident before finishing the third volume, which was completed by Allan Brooks. His collected papers and much artwork are archived and displayed at Cornell University. A young Roger Tory Peterson met Fuertes and admired his work. And David Sibley, acclaimed author of a contemporary field guide, *The Sibley Guide to Birds*, "spent hours staring at . . . the work of Fuertes" in his youth.[16]

Notes

Emily Dickinson, *The Complete Poems of Emily Dickinson*, ed. Thomas H. Johnson (Boston: Little, Brown and Company, 1960), J143.

1. The illustrations by Mark Catesby in this book can be found in Henrietta McBurney, *Mark Catesby's Natural History of America: The Watercolors from the Royal Library, Windsor Castle*, a catalogue for a traveling exhibition organized by the Royal Library, Windsor Castle, in conjunction with the Museum of Fine Arts (Houston: The Museum of Fine Arts; London: Merrell Holberton Publishers Ltd., 1997).

2. Scott Weidensaul, *Of a Feather: A Brief History of American Birding* (Orlando, Fla.: Harcourt Books, 2007), 20.

3. The illustration of the robin, wood thrush, and nuthatches in this book came from Alexander Wilson, *American Bird Engravings: All 103 Plates from American Ornithology* (New York: Dover Publications, 1975). See also, Alexander Wilson, *American Ornithology; or the Natural History of the Birds of the United States*, 9 volumes (Philadelphia: Bradford and Inskeep, 1808–1814). The goldfinch, blue jay, and Baltimore oriole are from *The Life and Letters of Alexander Wilson*, edited by Clark Hunter (Philadelphia: American Philosophical Society, 1983).

4. The illustrations by John James Audubon in this book came from *Audubon's Birds of America, Containing All the Original Prints, Reprinted from the First Royal Octavo Edition* (San Diego: Thunder Bay Press, 1994). See also, John James Audubon, *The Birds of America*, 4 volumes (London, 1827–1838).

5. Alice Ford, ed., *Audubon by Himself* (Garden City, N.Y.: Natural History Press, 1969), 3.

6. The illustrations in this book are from Thomas Nuttall, *A Manual of the Ornithology of the United States and Canada*, vol. 1 (Cambridge, Mass.: Hilliard and Brown, 1832) by courtesy of the Marine Biological Laboratory Woods Hole Oceanographic Institution Library; and from Nuttall, *A Popular Handbook of the Birds of the United States and Canada*, new, revised, and annotated edition by Montague Chamberlain (Boston: Little, Brown, and Company, 1903).

7. Weidensaul, *Of a Feather*, 86.

8. William J. Linton, *The History of Wood Engraving in America* (Boston, Mass., Estes and Lauriat, 1882), 10. Most of my information on John H. Hall came from this source.

9. The illustrations by Robert Ridgeway in this book came from Spencer F. Baird, Thomas M. Brewer, and Robert Ridgway, *A History of North American Birds* (Boston: Little, Brown and Company, 1875), vols. 1 and 2.

10. Weidensaul, *Of a Feather*, 130–31.

11. Christine E. Jackson, *Dictionary of Bird Artists of the World* (Woodbridge, Suffolk, England: Antique Collectors' Club Ltd., 1999), 409–10.

12. The two Cordelia Stanwood photographs included in this book are scans of photographs made from the original glass plates, by courtesy of The Stanwood Homestead Museum, Birdsacre, Ellsworth, Maine.

13. Chandler S. Richmond, *Beyond the Spring: Cordelia J. Stanwood of Birdsacre* (Ellsworth, Maine: The Latona Press, 1978; and Downeast Graphics and Printing Inc. 2008).

14. The illustrations in this book by Allan Brooks came from Edward Howe Forbush, *Birds of Massachusetts and Other New England States*, vol. 3 (Norwood, Mass.: Norwood Press, 1929). By courtesy of the Commonwealth of Massachusetts.

15. The illustrations in this book by Louis Agassiz Fuertes came from ibid., vol. 2.

16. David Allen Sibley, *The Sibley Guide to Birds* (New York: Knopf, 2000); Weidensaul, *Of a Feather*, 219.

Acknowledgments

The poems in this book are reprinted by permission of the publishers and the Trustees of Amherst College from *The Poems of Emily Dickinson*, Thomas H. Johnson, ed., Cambridge, Mass.: The Belknap Press of Harvard University Press, Copyright ©1951, 1955, 1979, 1983 by the President and Fellows of Harvard College. We thank Scarlett R. Huffman for her efforts in responding to our request. Without permission to use these poems, our book would not have been possible.

Our introduction to this selection of Dickinson poems includes a parallel theme of birding in the nineteenth century. This history, and the poems, are accompanied and enriched by the work of early artist/ornithologists. We have many people to thank for making these beautiful illustrations available.

Katie Holyoak at the Royal Collection, Picture Library, London, England, helped with permission to use the two Mark Catesby watercolors. They are from The Royal Collection ©2005, Her Majesty Queen Elizabeth II.

Michael Gold, Department of Agricultural Resources for the Commonwealth of Massachusetts, worked unflaggingly to make it possible for us to reproduce the splendid Louis Agassiz Fuertes and Allan Brooks paintings from Edward Howe Forbush's *Birds of Massachusetts and Other New England States*, published by the Commonwealth of Massachusetts in 1927 and 1929.

We would like to thank Gail Press and Ellen Milionis of World Publications Group, Inc., who graciously allowed us to use illustrations from *Audubon's Birds of America, Containing All the Original Prints Reprinted from the First Royal Octavo Edition*, by John James Audubon. Susan Burrell, at Dover Publications, smoothed the way for us to reproduce an illustration from their book *American Bird Engravings, All 103 Plates from American Ornithology*, by Alexander Wilson. Mary McDonald researched our request and helped secure permission from the Philadelphia American Philosophical Society to use a plate from *The Life and Letters of Alexander Wilson*, edited by Clark Hunter. The color plates in that book were also taken from Wilson's *American Ornithology*.

We especially wish to thank Diane Richmond Castle, Stan Richmond, and Grayson Richmond for their warm welcome at the Cordelia J. Stanwood Homestead Museum in Ellsworth, Maine. They helped a great deal with our research and graciously gave permission to use two of Stanwood's photographs in this book, as well as assisting us in our work with the old and out-of-print ornithology volumes in her collection. This effort brought to light Robert Ridgway's lithographs, four of which are reproduced in this book.

Patricia Zline, of Rowman and Littlefield Publishers, Inc., helped make it possible to use the lovely old photo of Emily Dickinson's home in Amherst, from Emily Dickinson: The Human Background of her Poetry, by Josephine Pollitt, first published by Harper and Brothers Publishers in 1930.

Patricia Cantwell Keene, Associate Director of Thorndike Library at the College of the Atlantic, helped immeasurably by suggesting that we could find copies of rare books on line, and by helping with research in their special collections. Internet Archive made it possible for us to view rare books in their digital collection.

The digital image of John H. Hall's "Ruby-Throated Humming-Bird" from A Manual of the Ornithology of the United States and Canada by Thomas Nuttall was graciously provided by the Marine Biological Laboratory Woods Hole Oceanographic Institution Library. Their generosity in sharing their holdings in the Rare Book Room is a great service to the public.

Marc Schuman made himself available at all hours for help in solving computer problems, and for untangling the snarls created by a neophyte user. His assistance in working with the illustrations was also invaluable. We are grateful for his expertise and patience.

Betty Miles read the manuscript and gave new life to our project. Jessica Oesterheld, Mark Mahnke, and Jean Converse, fellow birders, also read the manuscript early on and encouraged this endeavor. Others who have helped our effort are Eleanor Singer, Anaïs Salibian, Dia Lawrence, and Catherine Flannery.

We wish to thank the staff at Wesleyan University Press for help in seeing this book through to completion, and we are especially grateful to Suzanna Tamminen, Editor-in-Chief, who greeted the project with enthusiasm. Her involvement, patience, and expertise have greatly enhanced the creation of this book.

We are grateful for the dedicated staff at the University Press of New England. Eric Brooks was meticulous in overseeing the reproduction of the illustrations from old books and patient with our anxious inquiries concerning these lovely works of art. We thank Elizabeth Brash, skilled and reassuring production editor, who coordinated the design and production of the book. We are also indebted to April Leidig-Higgins: her lovely book and jacket designs underscore the beauty of the poems and illustrations. Rachael Cohen, copyeditor, ferreted out errors and added expertise to the flow of the manuscript.

Above all, as well as for their help with editing and technical problems, we are deeply thankful for the love and encouragement we have received from our families.

Bibliography

Audubon, John James. *Audubon's Birds of America, Containing All the Original Prints, Reprinted from the First Royal Octavo Edition.* Originally published in 1839–1844. San Diego: Thunder Bay Press, 1994.

Baird, Spencer F., Thomas M. Brewer, and Robert Ridgway. *A History of North American Birds, Land Birds,* 3 vols. Boston: Little, Brown, and Company, 1875.

Bailey, Florence Merriam. *Birds through an Opera Glass.* New York: Chautauqua Press, 1889.

Catesby, Mark. *The Natural History of Carolina, Florida and the Bahama Islands.* 2 vols. London: Printed for the author, 1731–1747.

Dickinson, Emily. *The Complete Poems of Emily Dickinson.* Edited by Thomas H. Johnson. Boston: Little, Brown, and Company, 1960.

———. *The Letters of Emily Dickinson.* Edited by Thomas H. Johnson. 3 vols. Cambridge, Mass.: Belknap Press of Harvard University Press, 1958.

———. *The Poems of Emily Dickinson.* R. W. Franklin, editor. Cambridge, Mass.: Belknap Press of Harvard University Press, 2005.

Farr, Judith. *The Gardens of Emily Dickinson.* Cambridge, Mass.: Harvard University Press, 2004.

Forbush, Edward Howe. *Birds of Massachusetts and Other New England States.* 3 vols. Norwood, Mass.: Norwood Press, 1927, 1929.

Ford, Alice, ed. *Audubon by Himself.* Garden City, N.Y.: Natural History Press, 1969.

Gibbons, Felton, and Deborah Strom. *Neighbors to the Birds: A History of Birdwatching in America.* New York: W.W. Norton, 1988.

Grosvenor, Gilbert, and Alexander Wetmore. *The Book of Birds.* 2 vols. Washington, D.C.: National Geographic, 1937.

Hart, Ellen Louis, and Martha Nell Smith, eds. *Open Me Carefully: Emily Dickinson's Intimate Letters to Susan Huntington Dickinson.* Ashfield, Mass.: Paris Press, 1998.

Hunter, Clark, ed. *The Life and Letters of Alexander Wilson.* Philadelphia: American Philosophical Society, 1983.

Jackson, Christine E. *Dictionary of Bird Artists of the World.* Woodbridge, Suffolk, England: Antique Collectors' Club Ltd., 1999.

Internet Archive. www.archive.org.

Kastner, Joseph. *A Species of Eternity.* New York: Alfred A. Knopf, 1977.

———. *A World of Watchers.* New York: Alfred A. Knopf, 1986.

Linton, William James. *The History of Wood-Engraving in America.* Boston: Estes and Lauriat, 1882.

McBurney, Henrietta. *Mark Catesby's Natural History of America: The Watercolors from the Royal Library, Windsor Castle.* Houston: The Museum of Fine Arts, and London: Merrell Holberton Publishers Ltd., 1997.

Mynott, Jeremy. *Birdscapes: Birds in Our Imagination and Experience.* Princeton, N.J.: Princeton University Press, 2009.

Nuttall, Thomas. *A Manual of the Ornithology of the United States and Canada.* 2 vols. Cambridge, Mass.: Hilliard and Brown, 1832, 1934.

———. *A Popular Handbook of the Birds of the United States and Canada.* Originally published by Little, Brown, and Company in 1891. New edition revised and annotated by Montague Chamberlain. Boston: Little, Brown, and Company, 1903.

Peterson, Roger Tory. "What Are You Really." In *All Things Reconsidered: My Birding Adventures.* Edited by Bill Thompson III. New York: Houghton Mifflin, 2006. Reprinted from *Bird Watcher's Digest* (March/April 1984).

Pollitt, Josephine. *Emily Dickinson: The Human Background of Her Poetry.* New York: Harper & Brothers Publishers, 1930.

Richmond, Chandler S. *Beyond the Spring: Cordelia J. Stanwood of Birdsacre.* Ellsworth, Maine: The Latona Press, 1978. New and revised edition, Ellsworth, Maine: The Latona Press, 1989; and Downeast Graphics and Printing, Inc. 2008.

Ridgway, Robert. *A Nomenclature of Colors for Naturalists, and Compendium of Useful Knowledge for Ornithologists.* Boston: Little, Brown, and Company, 1886.

Sibley, David Allen. *The Sibley Guide to Birds.* New York: Knopf, 2000.

Taverner, Percy A. *Birds of Western Canada.* Ottawa: F. A. Acland, 1926.

Weidensaul, Scott. *Of A Feather: A Brief History of American Birding.* Orlando, Fla.: Harcourt Books, 2007.

Wilson, Alexander. *American Bird Engravings: All 103 Plates from American Ornithology.* New York: Dover Publications, 1975.

Illustration Credits

"A View from the East of the Dickinson Home as It Appears Today," by an unknown photographer, is from Josephine Pollitt, *Emily Dickinson: The Human Background of Her Poetry* (New York: Harper & Brothers Publishers, 1930).

"Six Little Chickadees" and "Hermit Thrush Nest with Four Eggs and Bunchberry," photographs by Cordelia J. Stanwood, are courtesy of the Cordelia J. Stanwood Homestead Museum, Birdsacre, Ellsworth, Maine.

"Common Blue Bird and Great Mullein; American Robin or Migratory Thrush and Chestnut Oak"; "Wandering Rice-bird and Red Maple"; "Great Horned Owl"; "Baltimore Oriole or Hang-nest and Tulip Tree"; "Meadow Starling or Meadow Lark and Yellow-flowered Gerardia"; "Whip-poor-will and Black Oak"; "Great Carolina Wren and Dwarf Buck-eye"; and "Common American Crow and Black Walnut" by John James Audubon, are from *Audubon's Birds of America, Containing All the Original Prints, Reprinted from the First Royal Octavo Edition* (San Diego: Thunder Bay Press, 1994), courtesy of World Publications Group, Inc.

"Wood Thrush, Red-breasted Thrush or Robin, White-breasted Black-capped Nuthatch, and Red-bellied Black-capped Nuthatch" by Alexander Wilson, is from Alexander Wilson, *American Ornithology; or The Natural History of the Birds of the United States* (Philadelphia: Bradford and Inskeep, 1808), plate 2, vol. 1, and reprinted in *American Bird Engravings, All 103 Plates from American Ornithology* (New York: Dover Publications, Inc., 1975), with permission from Dover Publications, Inc.

"Blue Jay, Yellow-bird or Goldfinch, and Baltimore Bird" by Alexander Wilson, is from *American Ornithology*, plate 1, vol. 1; and *The Life and Letters of Alexander Wilson*, edited by Clark Hunter, through the Courtesy of the Philadelphia American Philosophical Society.

"Orchard Oriole, Baltimore Oriole, and Meadow Lark"; "Northern Pileated Woodpecker and Yellow-bellied Sapsucker"; and "Ruby-throated Hummingbird and Blue Vervain" by Louis Agassiz Fuertes, are from Edward Howe Forbush, *Birds of Massachusetts and Other New England States*, vol. 2

Index

Index of First Lines

ABOUT THE AUTHORS

EMILY DICKINSON is one of America's most celebrated early modern poets. Born in Amherst, Massachusetts in 1830, Dickinson wrote almost eighteen hundred poems throughout her lifetime. Shy and reclusive, Dickinson published very little during her lifetime, and the vast majority of her work did not appear until after her death in 1886.

JO MILES SCHUMAN is an avid birder and poetry reader. She is the author of *Art From Many Hands, Multicultural Art Projects* (1981, 2002), and she lives in Phippsburg, Maine.

JOANNA BAILEY HODGMAN has enjoyed a lifelong interest in reading and writing poetry. A retired English teacher, she lives in Rochester, New York.

ABOUT THE DRIFTLESS SERIES

The Driftless Series is a publication award program established in 2010 and consists of five categories:

DRIFTLESS NATIONAL, for a second poetry book by a United States citizen
DRIFTLESS NEW ENGLAND, for a poetry book by a New England author
DRIFTLESS ENGLISH, for English language poetry from an author outside the United States
DRIFTLESS TRANSLATION, for a translation of poetry into English
DRIFTLESS CONNECTICUT, for an outstanding book in any field by a Connecticut author

The Driftless Series is funded by the Beatrice Fox Auerbach Foundation Fund at the Hartford Foundation for Public Giving. For more information and a complete list of books in The Driftless Series, please visit us online at http://www.wesleyan.edu/wespress/driftless.